Build Your Own Website

Robert L. Perry

Watts LIBRARY

Franklin Watts
A Division of Grolier Publishing
New York • London • Hong Kong • Sydney
Danbury, Connecticut

To my wife Marilyn
For her steadfast support and faith

I wish to express my gratitude to Jamie L. Spriggs, a Campus Computing Associate at the University of Maryland, College Park, and my stepson Brian J. Dolbeare for their invaluable help in preparing this book. Jamie, who combines state-of-the-art technical knowledge with studies in Medieval French Literature, taught me the basics of HTML programming and gave me sound advice on the book's structure. Brian, who designs web pages for a major corporation, solved—in five minutes—a nagging problem that experts from a leading Internet company overlooked for almost a month.

Note to readers: Definitions for words in **bold** can be found in the Glossary at the back of this book.

Photographs ©: International Stock Photo: 36 (Michael Agliolo), 18 top left (Tom O'Brien), 18 bottom (Patrick Ransey), 18 top right (Valder/Tormey); Monkmeyer Press: 38 (Kerbs), 7 (Kopstein); Myron Jay Dorf: cover; PhotoEdit: 31 (Richard Lord), 8, 9 (Michael Newman); Stock Boston: 3, 40 (Daemmrich), 18 top center (John Eastcott/YVA Momatiuk); The Stock Market: 18 center (Julie Nicholls); Tony Stone Images: 12 (Edouard Berne).

Visit Franklin Watts on the Internet at:
http://publishing.grolier.com

Library of Congress Cataloging-in-Publication Data

Perry, Robert L. (Robert Louis), 1950–
    Build Your Own Website / Robert L. Perry
       p.   cm.— (Watts Library)
    Includes bibliographical references and index.
    Summary: Explains how to build and manage a website with instructions and codes in programming language called HTML (Hypertext Markup Language).
    ISBN 0-531-11756-1 (lib. bdg.)   0-531-16469-1 (pbk.)
    1. Web sites—Design—Juvenile literature. [1. Web sites.] I. Title. II. Series.
TK5105.888 P4235 2000
005.7'2—dc21

99-088786
CIP

Contents

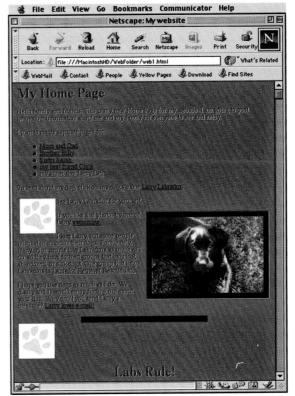

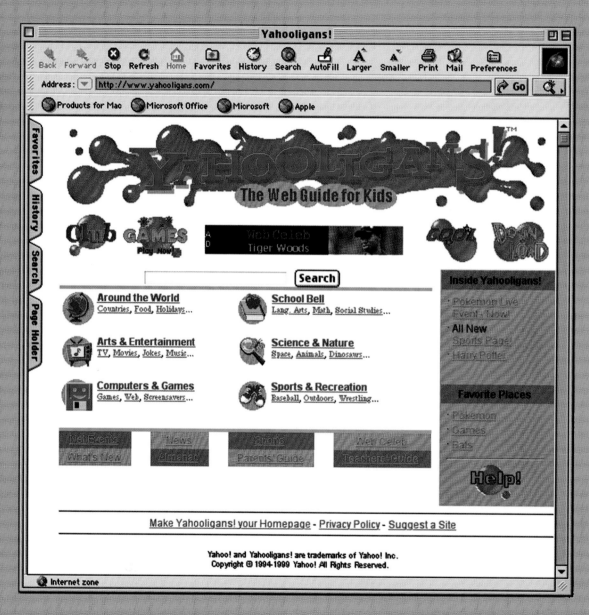

Here is an example of a website for Yahooligans.

Chapter One

Websites and Home Pages

The **Internet** is a huge computer network of machines that connect different computers around the world to one another. The **World Wide Web**, which is a part of the Internet, consists of websites that contain information about businesses, schools, organizations, and individuals. The World Wide Web allows anyone with a personal computer and a communications device to share information and programs and communicate easily and quickly. Websites can store all kinds of information, including programs, words, graphics, pictures, photographs, even cartoons, music, and videos.

What Is a Website?

An electronic document that you can access on the web is called a **web page**. A collection of web pages with a common purpose is called a **website**, and the first page of a website is called a **home page**. Think of a home page like home plate in baseball—all the action starts and ends there.

This book shows you how to create your own home page; build colorful, exciting, useful web pages; and master your own website in hours. You may think that doing this requires you to learn complex computer languages and use expensive computer equipment. That's not the case. In this book, you'll learn how to build and manage your own website with simple instructions and codes in an easy programming language called **HTML** (Hypertext Markup Language).

To prepare your web pages, you need only a standard personal computer and a simple writing program called a **text editor**. If you don't own a computer, you may be able to use one with a text editor at your school or library. To post your site on the World Wide Web, that is, make your site available to the millions of people who access the web, you need a communications device called a **modem**—which your computer may already have. A modem (short for MO-dulator-

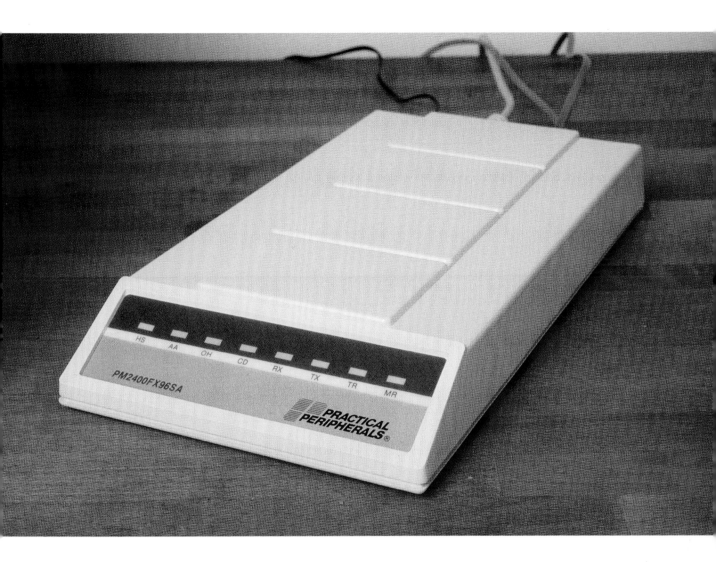

DEModulator) changes telephone signals into computer signals and vice versa.

You will also need a **web browser** application to view your web pages and **FTP (file transfer protocol)** software to upload (copy the file) to the web server. A web browser translates your simple HTML codes, text, and graphics into

You need a modem on your computer to post your website on the Internet.

7

You can tell if you have Internet Explorer if you see an opening screen like this one.

colorful web pages and connects you to the web. Internet Explorer and Netscape Navigator are a couple of the more well-known web browsers used today. A **web server** is a dedicated computer that stores web pages and sends them to peo-

ple when they use their web browsers to ask for web pages. The server is usually provided by an **Internet Service Provider** (ISP), a company that stores websites and provides you with access to them.

However, if you see a screen like this one, then you have Netscape Navigator.

If you type in the URL kidsdomain.com, you'll go to this website.

This is an example of a URL

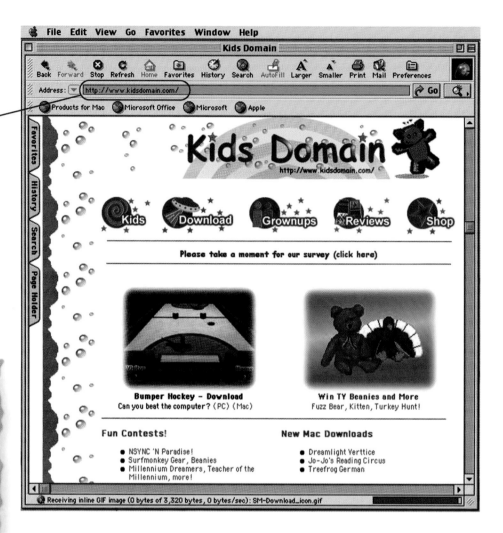

Your Login Name

See an adult or a teacher to provide you with an Internet account login name and password if your web browser or FTP application is not able to connect to a website or web server.

Your site—and each page—has a unique address called a **Uniform Resource Locator (URL)**. A URL consists of specific information that you type in so that your browser can find places on the Internet. People who know your URL can use their computers, web browsers, and modems to connect to your site.

For example, suppose that you create a site called "Cool Family." Then the URL could look like this: *http://www .coolfamily.com*. On your website, you can post a family newsletter, family pictures, articles, and **links** (connections) to your favorite websites. You can share your URL with your relatives, friends, teachers, and classmates. Then, with your site posted on a web server, they can access your site, view the pages, and swap messages with you. Even more amazing, anyone anywhere in the world can do the same thing. All this begins with simple HTML commands.

How to Pronounce URL

You pronounce **URL** with the letters "U-R-L," not like the man's name "Earl."

The Internet connects people all over the world with one another.

Chapter Two

Introducing HTML

When you "surf the web," that is, use a browser to connect to the World Wide Web, you can find fantastic things in cyberspace, for example, information about almost everything, colorful photographs, eye-catching graphics, cool music and sounds, and even videos. Yet, all these elements are created with the same basic tools—with a text editor and easy HTML commands. You can learn the basic codes and begin designing your own web pages in just hours.

Tags—They're It

HTML is a standard language created for web page design. A **tag** is part of the HTML language. The browser reads the tags and converts the information into what you see when you view the web pages. A tag controls every word, color, shape, photo, and sound you see on a web page. A group of tags makes up an HTML program that tells your browser how your page should look. For example, in HTML, a <b> tag tells the browser to boldface the text.

Tags are usually words (<title> for title) or short abbreviations (<b> for bold, <p> for new paragraphs, and so on). To separate tags from regular letters and words, they are placed between **angle brackets** (< = begin a tag, and > = end a tag). Every tag must have both brackets to give a command: for example, <i> = *italic text*.

You must have a pair of tags for every command: an opening tag and a closing tag. Every time you begin with an opening tag—<b> for bold—you have to add an ending tag with a backslash before the letter or word—</b>—when you want to stop the command. The backslash tells the browser that it is an ending tag.

For example, without the ending tag after <b> **the text would continue in boldface forever, but when you add the** </b> ending tag, the boldface stops and the text changes back to its normal appearance. Remember, all tags must include an opening and closing tag in order to work properly.

Types of Tags

To help you make your web pages interesting and colorful, different types of HTML tags have been developed, including the following types:

- **Format**. These tags control the text and page layouts. The simplest one is <p> to start a new paragraph. Other formatting tags create different types of lists, insert line breaks, and add other layout functions.
- **Text appearance**. These tags govern the font, size, style, and color of any text. The most common are <b> for **boldface**, <i> for *italics*, and <h1-6> for the size of the heading. You can also use tags to format the title for your web page, for example <title>.
- **Hyperlinks**. Using **anchor tags**, a hyperlink (also called a link) connects your web pages to other web pages or electronic mail. Anchor tags begin with <a followed by additional information> and close with <a/>. For example, <a href="http://www.4kids.org"> is a hyperlink to a home page with hundreds of links to interesting, safe sites for kids.

Case Doesn't Matter

Tags are not case sensitive so you can use either<b> or <B>, <i> or <I>, etc.

Choosing Head Size

Heading Sizes VARY. HTML lets you choose from six heading sizes. The tag <h1> is the largest, while <h6> is the smallest. The header tags do not need an ending tag.

Here is the source code for the website that we're creating as an example.

```
<html>
<body bgcolor=#FFCC33>
<head>
<title>My Web Site</title>
<!-- I can't believe I'm really doing this so easily -->
</head>
<body>
<H1><I>My Home Page</I></H1>
<p>Hello family and friends. this is my new <b>Home Page</b> for my Web site. I am going
to post interesting information about you and me for everyone to see and enjoy.
<p>I plan to create separate pages for Mom and dad, Billy and Sarah, and Larry the
Labrador.
</body>
</html>
<A HREF>anchor
```

This is the picture that will result from the source code that was shown above.

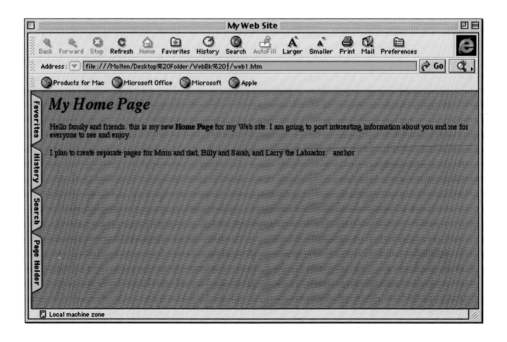

- **Images and Other Files**. These tags tell your **HTML document** to load a file that stores a photo, illustration, sound file, video clip, or text. The most common is <img src="filename"> for illustrations or photos. For example, if you insert a tag that reads <img src= "file:///MacintoshHD bluebird.jpg">, it would load a file located on your Macintosh hard drive named bluebird.jpg and display a photo of a bluebird on your web browser window.

At the end of this book, you can find a list of HTML tags that are used in this book. Now, you're ready to start writing and creating your own web pages.

Your website should represent your interests and talents that you want to share with the world.

Chapter Three

Let's Build a Website

Before you rush to create a web page, begin with a purpose and a plan. Keep your web page simple when you begin. After you finish your first page, you can learn advanced web design techniques, improve your existing pages, and add more information.

First, think about your purpose for a website. When that's clear, you'll know what to put on your pages. A website can do the following things:

- **Discuss your interests.** Post information, photos, and more about your sports, hobbies, pets, what you like, and even include things that you don't like.
- **Boast about your achievements**. Show off your awards, artwork, music, games, trophies, and anything you're proud of.
- **Organize family activities**. With a family newsletter and a family calendar, help your family keep track of important dates—like your birthday!—and activities—like your dance recital or a playoff game.
- **Reach out to relatives**. With a family reunion page, you can stay close to your grandparents, aunts and uncles, and cousins. You can include interesting information and pictures about family reunions and your relatives.
- **Help each other**. Create pages with links to school subjects, homework assignments, or topics you think are cool, such as adventure games or fashion.

Of course, you can do any or all of these activities, so choose one and get started.

Planning Your Site

When you know your purpose, plan your site with a "map," either an outline or a drawing—or both. It should show the basic layout and content for every page you plan to design.

With a clear purpose and a specific plan, you can begin creating your home page. First, create a new folder on your com-

WebFolder	
5 items, 1.9 GB available	
Name	**Date Modified**
image02.jpg	Today, 4:54 P
labphot5.jpg	Today, 4:42 P
larrylab.html	Today, 5:22 P
pawprnt	Today, 5:18 P
web1.html	Today, 5:42 P

Here is an example of a folder with html files and graphics stored in it.

puter. Store your final HTML and graphics files for your website in this folder. You can create a second folder to store your original text files, drafts, graphics, and so on.

Next, open your text editor so you can begin to write HTML code and text. Any simple text editor will work. If you have any version of Microsoft Windows, use Notepad. In Windows, click on "Start" and then click on "Programs." Next, click on "Accessories" at the top of that menu and then click on "Notepad" toward the bottom. If you use a Macintosh, use the SimpleText text editor in the Applications folder. Then create a new file, and you're ready to roll into HTML coding.

Creating Your Header

Every HTML page always begins with an <html> tag and ends with an ending </html> tag. Between these two tags, each page has two sections: the header and the body. For example, the header begins with <head> and ends with </head>. It includes information about the page that will not be displayed in the browser for everyone to see. Often, you will see the title (begin as <title> and end as </title>) that will appear in the browser window's title bar.

The header is also a good place to use the <!> or comment tag. Anything you write between the open angle bracket and an exclamation point (<!) and the close angle bracket (>) tag does not appear on your page. For example, <! -- I can't believe I'm really doing this so easily -- > will not appear on the page, but it will stay in your program. Comments help when you want to change a page later or to write a note to remember something.

Beginning and Ending a Page

After you close the header, you begin the body (<body>) and insert all of the text, tags, and links that you want on that page. You end the body information with </body>. When you have finished that page, remember that you must close it with </html>, or your browser will not know to end the page.

The body can contain as many lines of HTML tags as you like. However, the bigger your web page, the longer it will take to load. Try to use a combination of text and images that take up around one or two browser pages so that those who are viewing your page won't have to wait too long for it to load.

A Simple Web Page

Let's begin a simple HTML document that will become a web page. Type the following text into your new file:

```
<html>
<head>
<title>My website</title>
<! -- I can't believe I'm really doing this so easily -- >
</head>
<body>
<h1>My Home Page</h1>
<p>Hello family and friends. This is my new Home Page for my website. I am going to post interesting information about you and me for everyone to see and enjoy.
```

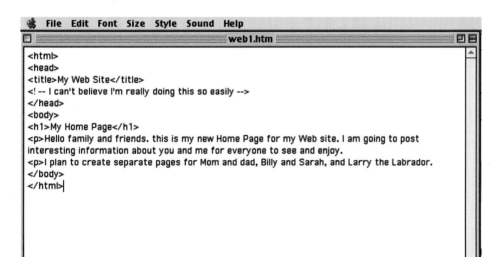

Writing source code for a website isn't as difficult as it may seem.

```
<p>I plan to create separate pages for Mom and Dad, Billy
and Sarah, and Larry the Labrador.
</body>
</html>
```

That's it. Congratulations, you've written your first HTML
program. Now, save two copies of this file in your drafts folder
or directory. Call the folder "webdraft" and the file "web1."
Save one copy as a standard Notepad text file with the **.txt**
extension (web1.txt). Save the second copy with the .HTML
extension (web1.htm). Make sure that you save the html file
with the .HTML or .HTM extension.

The Basic Tags

Did you notice how many basic HTML tags you've already
learned in this short example? You've learned the tags to open
and close a new web page, the header, the title, and the body
of the page, the main heading, and paragraphs. Now, let's see
what your page will actually look like when you post it on the
web. To do that, you need to open your web browser program.
The two most popular browsers are Netscape Navigator and
Microsoft Internet Explorer. This book relies on Netscape for
its examples.

In Netscape Navigator, on the menu bar at the top of the
main page, click on "File" or on a PC, press the ALT and F
keys at the same time and a menu pops up. Depending on the

version of Navigator you're using, look for "Open Page," "Open File," "Open File in Browser," or a similar command on this menu. Click on that. It will give you a blank area and ask you to enter a file name or location. Enter the name of your file on your hard drive, for example, c:\webdraft\ web1.html. Then press Return. On a Mac, navigate to the folder and file on your hard drive.

And there it is! Your first web page. But this is just the beginning. Soon, you will put photos and graphics and links to all kinds of interesting things on your page.

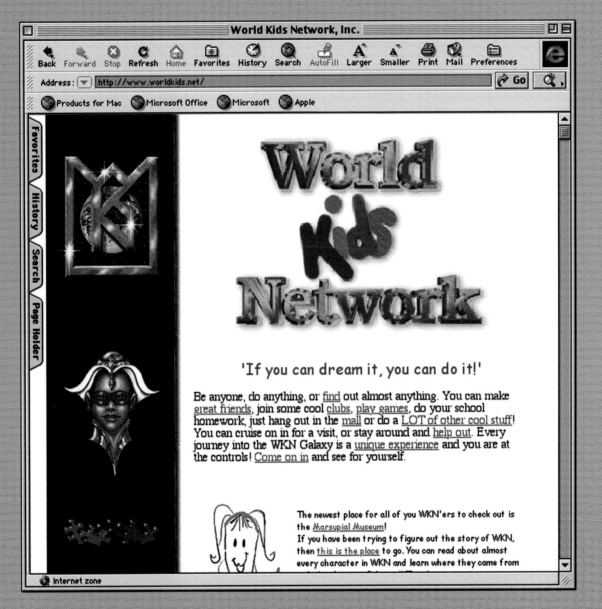

Links (colored and underlined words) can take you different places within a site if you click on them. However, sometimes links take you outside of the site to another website somewhere else on the Internet.

Chapter Four

Using Links and Anchors

When you use links and anchors to create web pages, you harness the power of the Internet so you can link your web pages to other files or pages anywhere. With these tags, you can link to anything, anywhere—from photos of your pets stored on your computer to an online game on a website in England.

What Is a Link?

A link is short for hypertext link or hyperlink. It is highlighted (usually in

The blue, underlined words are the links for the site we're making.

File   Edit   View   Go   Bookmarks   Communicator   Help

Netscape: My website

Back   Forward   Reload   Home   Search   Netscape   Images   Print   Security

Location: file:///MacintoshHD/WebFolder/web1.html   What's Related

WebMail   Contact   People   Yellow Pages   Download   Find Sites

My Home Page

Hello family and friends. This is my new Home Page for my website. I am going to post interesting information about me and my family for everyone to see and enjoy.

I plan to create separate pages for

- Mom and Dad
- Brother Billy
- Sister Sarah
- my best friend Chris
- my super dog Larry Lab

To read about my dog, click on my dog's name Larry Labrador.

See Larry Labrador for yourself.

If you like that photo, try one of Larry swimming.

I love Larry, but some people mistreat or abandon their dogs. Fortunately, many other people love Labradors as much as I do, so they have formed groups that help lost, abandoned, or sick dogs. One group that helps Labradors is Labrador Retriever Rescue, Inc.

I hope you like dogs as much as I do. We (Larry and I) would enjoy finding out about your dog. Why don't you send Larry a message? Larry loves e-mail!

Labs Rule!

blue) or underlined text on a page that controls a tag. The link tag retrieves a page either from the same website or another one. To retrieve the page, click on the link, and your computer calls the other website and loads the web page.

For example, notice the blue, underlined words "my super dog Larry Lab" on page 28. If you clicked on the blue words, a page of information about your dog would be retrieved from a file on your computer.

Anchors Away!

An anchor is the HTML tag (<A>) that opens and closes a link command. To add an anchor, you must insert a command into your HTML program. The program begins with an anchor or <A> (open angle bracket, A, close angle bracket). To use an anchor in the basic HTML program that you began in the last chapter, use the following steps.

1. Start the anchor with <A (open angle bracket, letter A, space).
2. Type in HREF followed by > to tell your computer to refer to the hypertext link.
3. Enter the path to and name of the file you want with quotation marks at each end. In this case, it could be as simple as "larrylab.html".
4. Enter the word or phrase that acts as the link you want people to click. In this case, it's "Larry Labrador."

5. Enter the ending anchor tag </A>.

Do *not* leave any space between Larry Labrador and the ending anchor tag. When you're done, your command should look like this if you saved the file in a folder named website on your C hard drive. Make sure that your path on your HTML matches the location of the original file on your website.

<A HREF="\larrylab.html">Larry Labrador</A>

To add this link to your page, just insert it where you want it to appear. The photo shows how the tag looks in your original program.

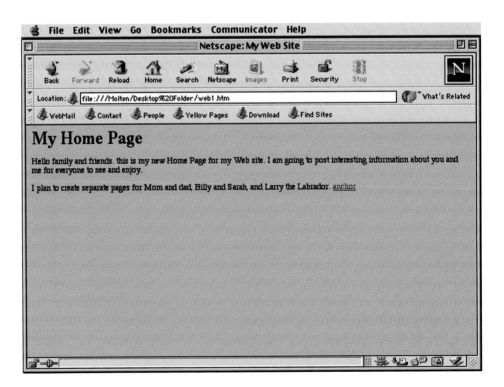

Here is how the tag should look in your program.

Adding an Image to Your Page

Suppose that you want to add a photo (called an image) of Larry to your page. An image can be a drawing, a graph, an illustration, or a photograph. You have to put your image in the correct file format. The two most common are called GIF (for graphical interchange format) and JPEG (for Joint Photographic Experts Group). You can use GIF for both drawings and photos. JPEG is better for photos because it can display deeper, richer colors.

One of the ways to add images is to scan them onto your computer with a scanner.

Scanning and Saving Images

To create an image file, you need two programs and a scanner. First, you need a graphics program that you can use to view your images. Second, you need a converter program that turns the image into either GIF or JPEG formats so that your HTML program can use it. Some packages include both programs so you may not have to worry about using two different programs.

31

What "IMG SRC" Means

In this command, "img" tells the browser to "put a graphic file here," and "src" tells it to find and display a graphic stored in that file.

Use Images from the Web with Caution

You can download thousands and thousands of graphics and photos from the web very easily. However, most of them are protected by a federal law called copyright. Unless the website says that the images are free for you to use, you may have to get permission from the website owner. Ask your parents for advice or use your own photos.

The scanner, attached to your computer, works like a photocopier, but it turns images into digital signals and stores them on a computer. After you scan your images into your graphics software and convert them to GIF or JPEG format, you can add a line to your HTML program that will load an image. You can write the program so that the image either loads automatically or works like a link.

Adding the Image Command

After you learn to use the highlighted link on your web pages, try both ways. First, here's how to load an image automatically:

1. Find a photo, a drawing, or a graphic you want to put on your page; scan and save it with your graphics program.
2. Save the image file in your website directory as c:\website\image01.gif.
3. In your HTML program, use the <IMG SRC> (or image source) tag.

<p><img src="image01.gif">

The basic command to load any image, graphic, or photo is <img src="filename">. And the <p> paragraph tag tells the program to begin on a new line.

An example of adding an image to a page is shown on page 28.

Adding a Photo Link

If you'd rather put your image on another page and save space on your home page, you can put the image on another web page and create a link to it from the first page. To add a link to the image, enter the tag for an anchor, followed by the path to the new web page.

<p>If you'd like to see a picture of Larry swimming, just click here <A HREF= "\larrylab.html">Larry Loves To Swim!</A>

Then, create a new web page for the image file and use the file name from the anchor we just created on the first web page. To add the image file to the new web page, use the "img src" html tag followed by the path to the image file. Be sure to use the path where the file will reside on your website.

<img src="image02.jpg">Larry Loves To Swim!

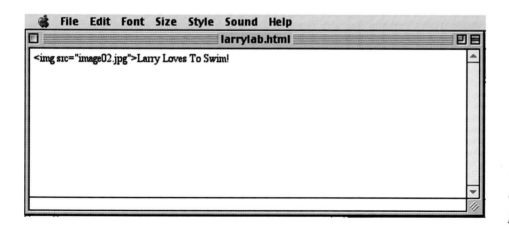

Use this code to create a link to another web page.

We've added a page to the website with an image of Larry Lab here.

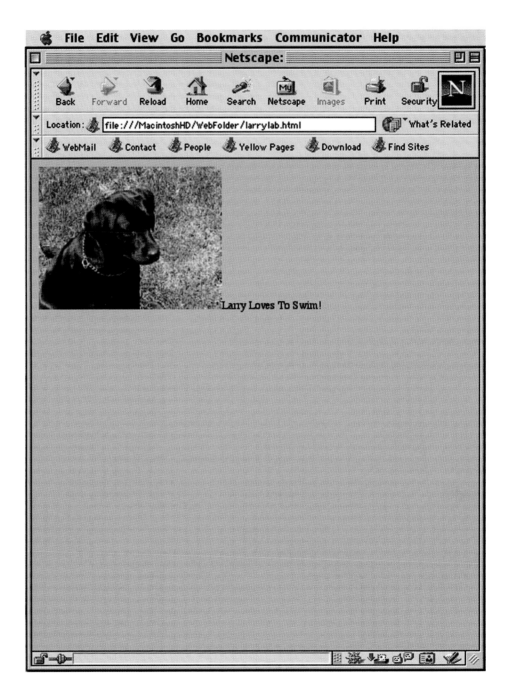

Adding a Hyperlink to Another Website

Although you can have fun with images and photos, you may want to help your visitors learn more about your favorite subjects. But you don't want to use your family's website to do that. Instead, you can add a true hypertext link to another website that tells them more about your interests.

For example, some groups help Labradors whose owners mistreat or abandon them. Other people should know about these groups, so you can add a link to those groups on your web pages. Here's how to do it:

1. Search the web with a search engine to find a Labrador rescue group.
2. When you find a group that you like or is near you, copy the group's URL (and bookmark it for easy reference).
3. Add the following text and hyperlink to your HTML program: <p>I love Larry, but some people mistreat or abandon their dogs. Fortunately, many other people love Labradors as much as I do, so they have formed groups that help lost, abandoned, or sick dogs. One group that helps Labradors is <A HREF=www.groupname>Labrador Retriever Rescue, Inc.</A>.

URLs can lead you to a wealth of new information that you might never have known existed otherwise.

Chapter Five

How to Find Your Website

After you create some web pages, it's not much fun if they only sit on your computer. You want your friends, classmates, and relatives to be able to find and enjoy your site. To do that, you need a real web address called a URL (Uniform Resource Locator). Every web page has its own unique URL just as everyone has a different social security number.

Posting Your Page on the Web

To post your web pages on the Internet, you need an FTP program that can upload your web files to an Internet Service Provider (ISP). The ISP actually stores your files and lets other people access them.

You'll need an FTP program to upload your web files to an Internet Service Provider.

You can find free or low-cost FTP programs on the web through sites that offer freeware (free programs anyone can use) and shareware (low-cost programs that may offer free trials). Two popular programs for Windows-based PCs are

WS-FTP and Cute FTP; for the Apple Macintosh, try FETCH and Anarchie.

Different ISPs have different ways to upload your programs, but generally it is easy. Your computer must have a modem, communications software, and a web browser. You also need to know the login and password for your ISP account. If your computer is on any internal web network, or an Intranet, you may need to know a password before you can access the web server you need to copy your web pages to.

Free Websites for Your Pages

Many ISPs and web hosts offer free space on their websites so you can share your pages on their sites with other people. Most ISPs also give you web authoring tools, programs, and tips on how to design web pages. They don't expect you to know how to program in HTML.

You should ask your parents for help because many sites with free web space may require young people to have their parents' permission.

Your Own Domain Name

Your family can have its own **domain name**. The steps are simple, but your family has to pay for it: prices range from $70 to $120 to register for the first two years and $35 to $60 each year after that. Prices vary according to registration services that are provided by the company you pay to register your domain name. After you register the name, you must store

Posting Your Web Page

Talk to an adult or a teacher if you need to find out how to post your web pages to a web server. When you copy your web pages to the server, remember the exact path to the folder on the server where your web pages are stored. Then type this path into your web browser as the URL to your web pages.

39

your site on an ISP. A website hosting account may cost $20 a month or more, plus additional fees. During late 1999, the domain name registration process was changing. Several companies register names, so go to *www.internic.net* for the most up-to-date information.

What good is your website if no one knows it exists? Make sure that you tell all your friends and relatives what your web address is so that they can see your website.

Get the Word Out

Whenever you "surf" the Internet, let people know about your site. Be sure that your parents know what you're doing and help you choose safe places. Try these other ways to let others know how to find your web page.

- Give everyone you know—your family, friends, and classmates—your URL.
- Write a letter or a short article about it for your school newspaper.
- Write a letter to the computer editor of your local newspapers.
- Do a science project about your site for your Science Fair.
- Ask your parents to tell the people they work with about your family site.
- Join a listserv, which is a group of people with shared interests.
- Join safe chatrooms and tell other kids your age about your site.
- Tell online educational or children's groups about it with electronic mail. They might put a link on their page to your site.

You and your fellow students can now learn more advanced HTML techniques.

Chapter Six

Having Fun with Your Website

Now that everyone on the Internet can access your website, you may want to learn more advanced HTML commands so that you and your visitors can have even more fun with your site.

When people visit a website, they often want to swap e-mail messages. If your family already has an e-mail address, you can add a simple link to your home page. Add the following HTML link with the "mailto" command to your program, rather than a file name or URL:

<A HREF=mailto:(e-mail address)>words you want highlighted</A>

You can insert any e-mail address you want and any highlighted words that make it more fun. If you want to encourage your visitors to swap messages about dogs, you could add a sentence to your page and ask them to send you (or your dog) an e-mail message. The HTML command line would look like this:

<A HREF="mailto:myemail@freemail.org">Larry Lab loves e-mail</A>

The HTML language gives you many more commands and codes so you, too, can create designs as colorful and entertaining as those you see when you visit other websites. Some are very simple, like <b> for boldface and <i> for italics. Use these *occasionally* to make your text stand out.

For example, you could add <b> every time before Larry Lab's name so it would stand out in each sentence, except for links. (The bold won't work on links). <b>Larry Lab</b> would look like this **Larry Lab**.

Colors Catch Attention

If lots of people visit your site, you want it to look good. Start with your headings and the screen display. You can change the default (normal) background color from a bland, grayish white to just about any color you want. To show any one of a number of standard colors, make a simple addition to the <body> command like this:

<body bgcolor=color>

The "bg" is an abbreviation for background. Try "yellow" as your background color. As the photo shows, it's a bit bright.

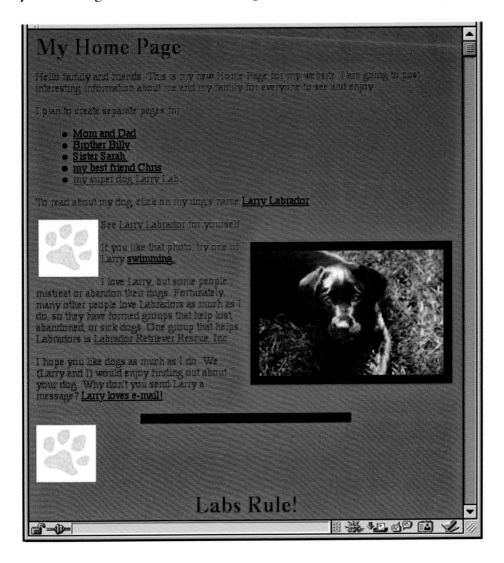

Here is what our final web page looks like. Impressive, isn't it?

Changing Header Tags

"Labs Rule!" may not stand out enough in regular text. With caution, you can add more tags and make it really stand out. For example, adding a header tag to "Labs Rule!" gives you a much bigger, bolder font size, like this:

<h3>Labs Rule!</h3>
Labs Rule!

The Center Command

That's bigger, but your browser starts every line in the far left margin. Instead, use other tags that realign your text or image. The <center> command does just that by putting text in the center of the page, so add it to your program like this:

center><h3>Labs Rule!</h3></center>
<div align="center">**Labs Rule!**</div>

Making a List, Checking It Twice

To make your page easy to read, you can use lists with bullets. Basic HTML lets you choose three types of lists: definition, numbered, and bulleted. Bullets are more fun because you can use three types of bullets: square, circle, or disc. For example, suppose that you want to list the members of your family on your home page and the links to their pages. Use the <ul> tag to begin an undefined list and the <li> tag before each item in the list. Add this to your HTML program:

```
<ul>
<li><A HREF="momanddad.html">Mom and Dad</A>
<li><A HREF="brother.html">Brother Billy</A>
<li><A HREF="sister.html">Sister Sarah<A/>
<li><A HREF="friend.html">my best friend Chris</A>
<li><A HREF="larrylab.html">my super dog Larry Lab</A>
</ul>
```

Inserting Easy Graphics

You can add graphics and align them as easily as you do photographs. Suppose that you want to add a dog graphic. Let's insert a paw print graphic and use the tags—IMAGE and ALIGN—to shift it and some text to the left.

```
<img align=left src="pawprnt">
```

Shifting Paragraphs

You can also use the ALIGN or CENTER tag to shift whole paragraphs with the <p> tag. For example, the <p align= center> command will let you center some lines and give your page a different look. Enter

```
<p align=center> How many laps would a Labrador leap
<p align=center> If a Labrador could leap laps?
```

And it would look like this:

How many laps would a Labrador leap
If a Labrador could leap laps?

Mistakes to Avoid with Web Pages

As you practice doing your own pages, you can find hundreds of ways to post tables, animation, cartoons, sounds and music, video clips, and more to your website. If you do too much, however, your site can become ugly, crowded, annoying, and slow. You should try to avoid these common mistakes:

- Pictures that are too large, too complex, or that take too long to download. Keep it simple and quick with one or two small images per page.
- Images that are constantly moving and text that distracts you.
- Dead-end or orphan pages that seem left out of nowhere. Always include a link back to the home page.
- Non-standard link colors should not be used because people are unfamiliar with them. Use the standard blue for links and red for clicked links.
- Long, scrolling pages that go on forever. People will scroll through some pages, but prefer to use links to avoid long pages.

Next Steps

So far, you've learned how to create your own web pages with HTML programs and even had some fun. Better yet, many websites help you create web pages and give you all the basic templates and formats.

If you want to learn advanced HTML programs, you can obtain programs called HTML editors that enter tags so you don't have to type all the letters all the time. Some ISPs provide HTML editors for free or at low cost, or you can buy them from the web or retail stores that sell software.

However, just like becoming a good athlete or musician, it's best if you learn and practice the basics so you can create your own excellent website for you and your family. Now, relax and enjoy the fun and creativity of becoming a webmaster.

Final Page Code

```
<html>
<head>
<title>My website</title>
</head>
<body bgcolor=#ffffff>
<body text=#00009c>
<body link=#8c1717>
<body alink=#6b4226>
<h1>My Home Page</h1>
<p>Hello family and friends. This is my new Home Page for my website. I am going to post interesting information about me and my family for everyone to see and enjoy.
<p>I plan to create separate pages for
<ul>
<li><A HREF="momanddad.html">Mom and Dad</A>
<li><A HREF="brother.html">Brother Billy</A>
<li><A HREF="sister.html">Sister Sarah<A/>
<li><A HREF="friend.html">my best friend Chris</A>
<li><A HREF="larrylab.html">my super dog Larry Lab</A>
</ul>
```

```
<p>To read about my dog, click on my dog's name
<A HREF="larrylab.html">Larry Labrador</A>.
<p><img align=left src="pawprnt">
<p>See <A HREF=labphot5.jpg>Larry Labrador</A> for
yourself.
<br>
<br>
<img align=right border=10 src="labphot5.jpg">
<p>If you like that photo, try one of Larry <A
HREF=labphot3.jpg>swimming.</A>
<p>I love Larry, but some people mistreat or abandon their
dogs. Fortunately, many other people love Labradors as
much as I do, so they have formed groups that help lost,
abandoned, or sick dogs. One group that helps Labradors is
<A HREF=http://www.lrr.org>Labrador Retriever Rescue,
Inc.</A>
<p>I hope you like dogs as much as I do. We (Larry and I)
would enjoy finding out about your dog. Why don't you
send Larry a message?
<A HREF=mailto:(e-mail address)>Larry loves e-mail!</A>
<br>
<br>
<hr noshade align=center size=10 width=50%><img
src="pawprnt">
<center><h1>LabsRule!</h1></center>
</body>
</html>
```

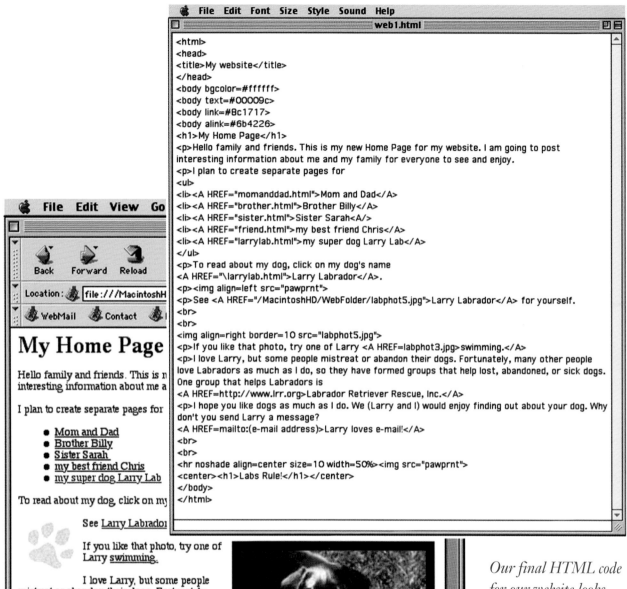

File Edit Font Size Style Sound Help

web1.html

```
<html>
<head>
<title>My website</title>
</head>
<body bgcolor=#ffffff>
<body text=#00009c>
<body link=#8c1717>
<body alink=#6b4226>
<h1>My Home Page</h1>
<p>Hello family and friends. This is my new Home Page for my website. I am going to post
interesting information about me and my family for everyone to see and enjoy.
<p>I plan to create separate pages for
<ul>
<li><A HREF="momanddad.html">Mom and Dad</A>
<li><A HREF="brother.html">Brother Billy</A>
<li><A HREF="sister.html">Sister Sarah<A/>
<li><A HREF="friend.html">my best friend Chris</A>
<li><A HREF="larrylab.html">my super dog Larry Lab</A>
</ul>
<p>To read about my dog, click on my dog's name
<A HREF="\larrylab.html">Larry Labrador</A>.
<p><img align=left src="pawprnt">
<p>See <A HREF="/MacintoshHD/WebFolder/labphot5.jpg">Larry Labrador</A> for yourself.
<br>
<br>
<img align=right border=10 src="labphot5.jpg">
<p>If you like that photo, try one of Larry <A HREF=labphot3.jpg>swimming.</A>
<p>I love Larry, but some people mistreat or abandon their dogs. Fortunately, many other people
love Labradors as much as I do, so they have formed groups that help lost, abandoned, or sick dogs.
One group that helps Labradors is
<A HREF=http://www.lrr.org>Labrador Retriever Rescue, Inc.</A>
<p>I hope you like dogs as much as I do. We (Larry and I) would enjoy finding out about your dog. Why
don't you send Larry a message?
<A HREF=mailto:(e-mail address)>Larry loves e-mail!</A>
<br>
<br>
<hr noshade align=center size=10 width=50%><img src="pawprnt">
<center><h1>Labs Rule!</h1></center>
</body>
</html>
```

File Edit View Go

Back Forward Reload

Location : file:///MacintoshH

WebMail Contact

My Home Page

Hello family and friends. This is n
interesting information about me a

I plan to create separate pages for

- Mom and Dad
- Brother Billy
- Sister Sarah
- my best friend Chris
- my super dog Larry Lab

To read about my dog, click on my

See Larry Labrador

If you like that photo, try one of Larry swimming.

I love Larry, but some people mistreat or abandon their dogs. Fortunately, many other people love Labradors as much as I do, so they have formed groups that help lost, abandoned, or sick dogs. One group that helps Labradors is Labrador Retriever Rescue, Inc.

I hope you like dogs as much as I do. We (Larry and I) would enjoy finding out about your dog. Why don't you send Larry a message? Larry loves e-mail!

Labs Rule!

Our final HTML code for our website looks like this.

List of HTML Tags Used in This Book

Defined in alphabetical order are all of the HTML tags or commands used to create web pages in this book.

`<! -- >`	comment tag for text that should not appear on your web page
`<A>`	anchor tag that begins a command to create a link to other files, pages, sites, locations on the same page
`<A HREF=>`	anchor tag with a command that creates a link
`<A HREF=mailto>`	anchor tag with command that creates an electronic mail link
`<B>`	boldface tag for text
`<BODY>`	tag that begins the actual web page content
` `	line break tag that skips a line on the page
`<CENTER>`	tag for centering anything in the middle of a page
`<H1> through <H6>`	heading tag that automatically sets the size of a heading

\<HEADER\>	tag that identifies the heading that will appear in the browser menu bar
\<HTML\>	tag that begins and ends (\</HTML\>) all web pages
\<I\>	italic tag that sets all text in italics
\<IMG ALIGN=page location\>	tag that puts a graphic, drawing, or photo at the left, right, middle, top, or bottom of a page
\<IMG SRC=file name\>	image tag that identifies the location of a graphic, drawing, or photo
\<LI\>	tag placed before each item on a list
\<P\>	tag that automatically skips a line between paragraphs and begins a new one
\<TITLE\>	tag that identifies the title of the web page but does not appear on the page
\<UL\>	tag that begins and ends an undefined or bulleted list

Glossary

Anchor—also called **anchor tag,** the HTML tag (<A>) that opens and closes a link command, in other words <A HREF=http://www.webaddress.com></A>

Angle brackets—the keyboard symbols < and > that you put around an HTML tag or command

Browser—also called a **web browser,** a communications program that allows a user to receive and send web pages on the Internet

Domain name—the legal, unique name for a website that is registered with an official agency that monitors website addresses

File transfer protocol (FTP)—an application that you use to transfer programs and web pages across the Internet

Home page—also spelled as one word (homepage); the first page on a website that introduces the site's contents to the visitor

HTML document—any data file with **Hypertext Mark-up Language** program commands that can be loaded as a web page with a web browser

Hypertext Mark-up Language (HTML)—the programming language with which you design and create web pages with plain language commands

Internet—a global network of computers that are connected so that each computer can communicate with every other computer on the network

Internet Service Provider (ISP)—an organization that provides access to the World Wide Web (WWW), information, and services to web users

Link—also called **hypertext link** or **hyperlink**, specially marked text (usually in red) or a symbol that connects one web page to another file or web page when you place the cursor on the symbol or text and single-click with a mouse

Modem—shortened version of MODulator-DEModulator, a communications device that translates telephone signals into computer signals and vice versa so personal computers can communicate across regular telephone lines

Tag—a plain language command in the HTML language that

determines what the text, symbols, and graphics on a web page look like

Text editor—a program with a limited number of commands that allows the user to create and modify written text

URL (Uniform Resource Locator)—the acronym, pronounced with the letters "U-R-L," for the specific web address and file name for any web page

Web page—a page of text, symbols, graphics, and more programmed in a hypertext mark-up language that is stored on a web server and can be displayed through a web browser

Web server—a central storage location for web pages and software that responds to requests for and displays those pages

Website—any single web page or collection of web pages with a common theme

World Wide Web (WWW)—a worldwide collection of files accessible by computers through the Internet that are connected by hyperlinks and communication networks

To Find Out More

Websites

Many Information Service Providers (ISPs) and web pages teach you HTML programming, give you free HTML editors, and even give you free space so that you and your family can build your own website. Here are some that I used to write this book:

4 Kids.Org
www.4kids.org
Site for children with hundreds of links called "Coolspots" to free information, graphics, etc. about web pages.

HTML Wizards
www.htmlwizards.com
HTML Wizards site for free advice, tutorials, software, and more for designing your own site.

Webmonkey

www.hotwired.com/webmonkey

Site with tutorials for learning HTML programing and much more.

New Zealand World Wide Access

www.nzwwa.com/mirror/clipart/

Site for numerous free illustrations, banners, animated graphics, buttons, and more.

KidsClick!

sunsite.berkeley.edu/KidsClick!

Extensive, safe site for children with links to computers and web page design.

National Geographic

www.nationalgeographic.com/kids/

Amazingly fun site filled with jokes, games, puzzles, books, and plenty of wonderful things for kids to do. It also has the traditional geographic facts available.

The Freesite.com

www.thefreesite.com

Site for free or low-cost graphics, banners, counters, HTML editors, web development tools, and more.

TheGlobe.com
www.theglobe.com
Site with extensive home page resources and links, as well as 12 MB of free space and templates to build your own pages.

Books

Gralla, Preston. Online Kids: *A Young Surfer's Guide to Cyberspace*. New York: John Wiley & Sons, 1996.

Pedersen, Ted, and Moss, Francis. *Internet for Kids*. New York: Price Stern Sloan, 1995.

Smith, Bud, Bebak, Arthur, and Werbach, Kevin. *Creating Web Pages for Dummies* (4th Ed.). Indianapolis: IDG Books Worldwide, 1999.

Taylor, Dave. *Creating Cool HTML 4 Web Pages*. Indianapolis: IDG Books Worldwide, 1998.

Wolff, Michael. *Kids Rule the 'Net*. New York: Wolff New Media, 1996.

A Note on Sources

You can find literally hundreds of books, magazine articles, and websites with information about how to create your own website. From this large number, I had to choose those sources best for children and found many websites for kids that explain the basics. I also interviewed several experts and children who had developed their own sites. They showed me the kinds of information that would be most useful to someone who knows a little about personal computers, but nothing about HTML programming and creating websites. Finally, some of the web hosts that let you create and post a website for free make it very simple to create a site and help teach you how to develop your own web pages.

Index

Numbers in *italics* indicate illustrations.

About the Author

Noted author Robert L. Perry has written about personal computers for more than 20 years. He wrote one of the first books about microcomputers for home use and has authored several other books about computers and computer-related careers for Franklin Watts, including *Computer Crime* and *Electronic Service Careers*. He teaches professional writing at the University of Maryland, College Park, has a master's degree in speech communication, and makes his home near Annapolis, Maryland.